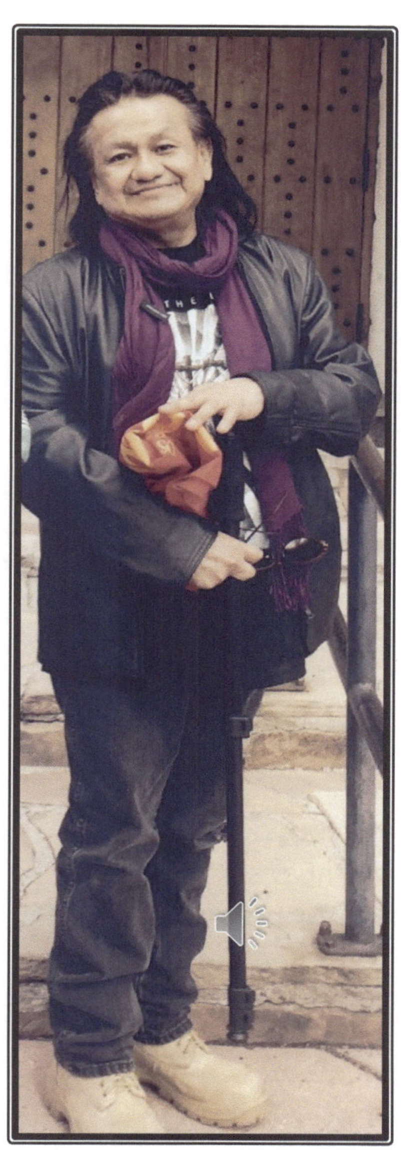

The Inspirational Art
of
David Dawangyumptewa

Katie McClain Richarme

Michael Richarme, Ph.D.

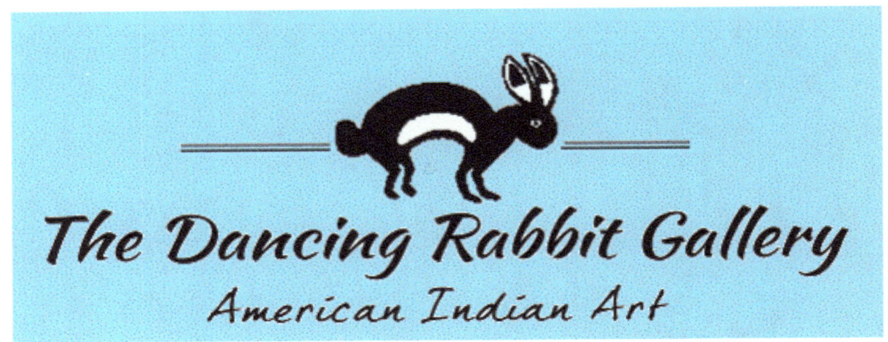

ISBN: 9798428541892
ISBN-13: 9798428541892

Library of Congress Control Number: 2022904688

Printed in The United States of America. Print year 2022.

Preface

David Dawangyumptewa is a very talented artist,
and in itself that would make this a wonderful story.

His ability to see the culture and traditions of his
Water Clan and of his Hopi people, and translate those
into vivid, emotional, and dynamic paintings, is quite
amazing.

This book, however, is about David's journey, his
courage, and his steadfast desire to educate and inspire
others about the Hopi Nation. His gentle nature is one
that soothes all who spend time with him, and his
stories of his journey on Mother Earth carry many
lessons for all of us.

David's last name in Hopi means the motion of the sun
as it rises in the east each morning.

An Artist Emerges

David began life in 1957 on the three mesas of the Hopi Nation. He went to boarding school with Navajo children, however, and learned immediately the differences between the gentle Hopi culture and the more aggressive Navajo culture.

David attended IAIA in Santa Fe, Haskell Institute in Kansas, and Norther Arizona University in Flagstaff. He painted different images and begin experimenting with perspective, colors, and imagery from his culture.

After his schooling was complete, David embarked on a profession of being a lighting technician for professional musicians. He traveled the country setting the lighting for musicians such as Linda Ronstadt, Jackson Browne, and Sting.

But then David returned to his first true love, painting.

A Voice Develops

The style and content of Dawangyumptewa's work are reflective of his Hopi background and Water Clan affiliation.

"The majority of my paintings are thought of as mythical or spiritual subject pieces. By allowing the viewer to play and expand their imagination, the discovery of a mystical environment in the mind's eye is the ultimate reason for creativity.

My paintings reveal a part of myself through consciously developed symbolism, as well as traditional regional life ways. These are images that tell of my loves- family relationships, religious upbringing and observations." – David Dawangyumptewa

Honan Mana

Arches of turquoise and coral suggest a cave opening with subtle strokes of what might be rushes at the entrance. Hopi maiden's mouth is open and her butterfly whirls are portrayed in beautiful turquoise and coral colors.

The heart line of the bear is a bright coral, suggesting the strength of his heart; the strength of the bear clan is very evident. Japanese gold leaf is scattered across the layered composition like sparkling stars.

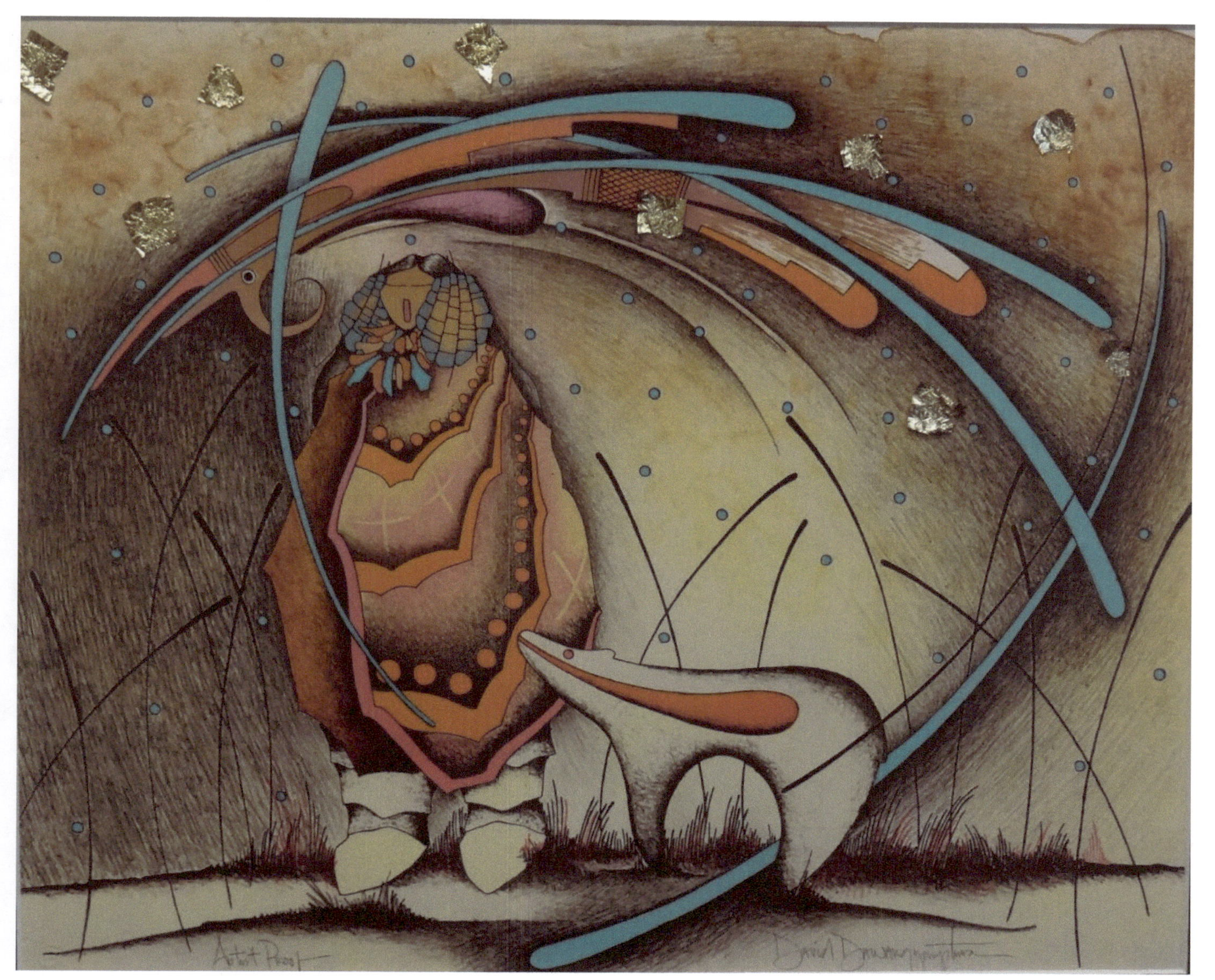

DR 563 - Honan Mana   1988
                                         15” by 18”

Arrival of the Water Clan

One of the most important stories of the Hopi migration is the account of flood and the arrival of the Water Clan to the mesas.

It was on the mesa and in the village of Walpi where the Water Clan offered their contribution to help bring rain and moisture for the people. This offering of water and rain is the primary content of The Arrival of the Water Clan.

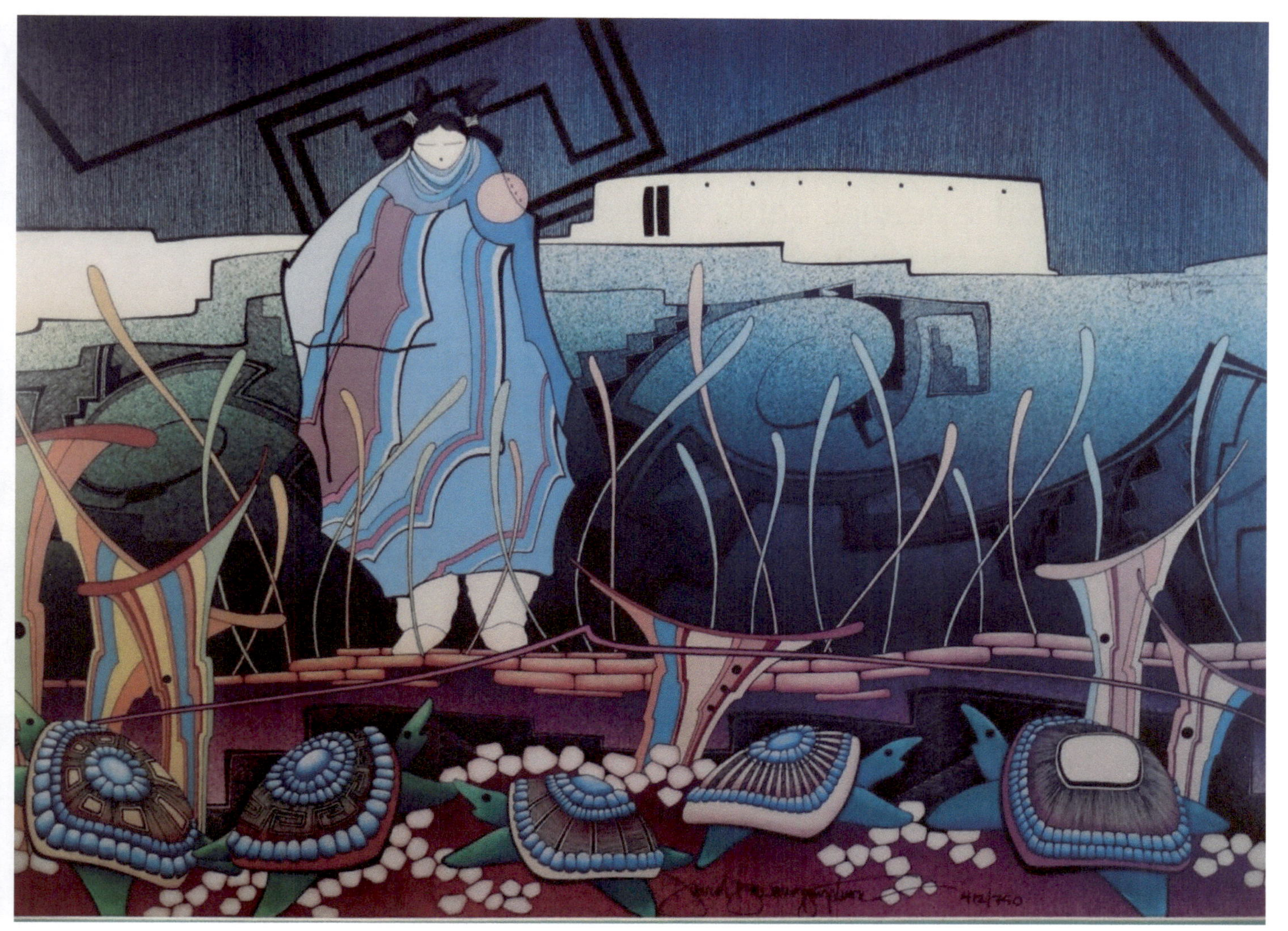

DR 536 - Arrival of the Water Clan   1988
26 ½" by 31 ½"

Polik Mana
Watching the Frogs Go By

Dragonflies dance behind the stalks of corn as Polik-Mana watches the brightly colored frogs go by.

The colors of this painting are so vibrant. The Polik-Mana, or Butterfly Maiden, although beautifully dressed is not really a katsina, but rather a dancer who appears in various Hopi ceremonies. Her attire usually includes a beautifully elaborate tablita headdress.

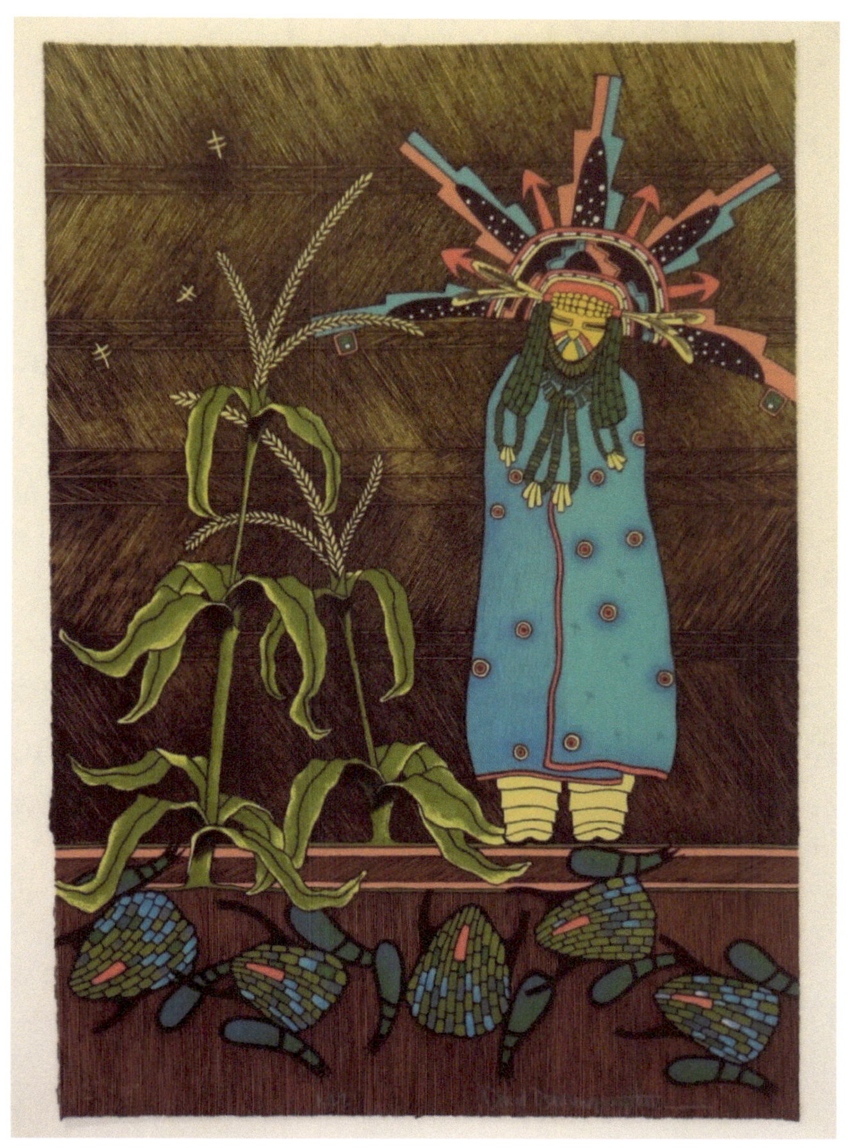

DR 573 - Polik Mana Watching The Frogs Go By   1984
24" by 17" Framed

Elements of the Earth

"Wrapped in her star blanket, this young maiden is among many design elements of the earth. The two-toned green skyband is over powered by all of the birds of the sky. Selected golden breath-bodies whisper words of wisdom as they radiate out of the depths of knowledge. Periwinkle moisture dew drops rise to the sky.

Do not make the waters angry as the consequences are threatening. Winds of change are at hand and the fires will consume the earth." David Dawangyumptewa

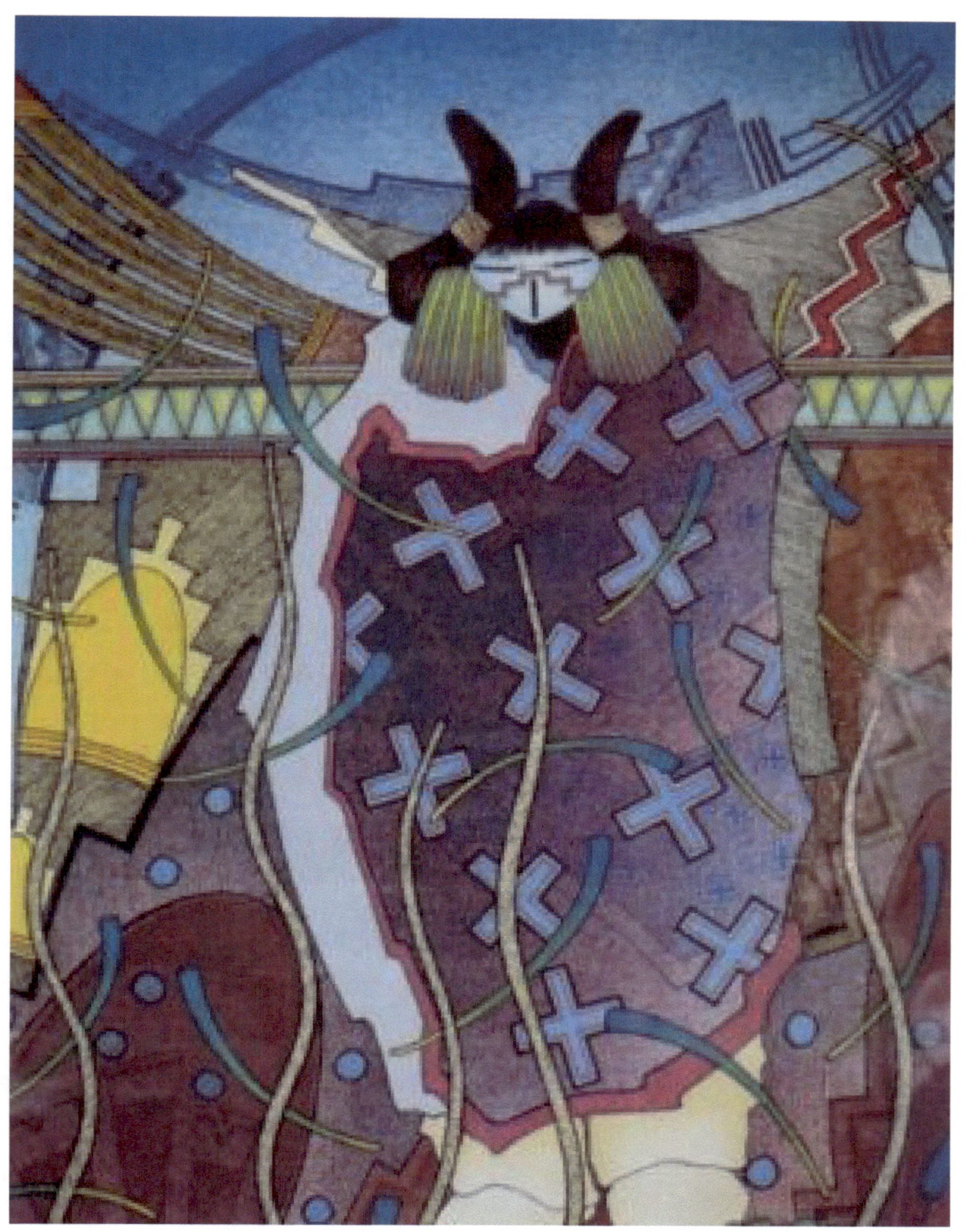

DR 586 - Elements of the Earth   1991
    31 ½" by 25 ½" double matted and framed

Sunset Song

Sunset Song focuses on the ending of the day as the world begins to glow in the beautiful colors of the setting sun against the darkening sky.

In this painting a lovely Hopi potter sings over a Hopi seed jar. She is wrapped in a simple manta and wears traditional white doe-skin moccasins and beautiful earrings. The polychrome seed jar is decorated with typical Sikyatki-revived designs.

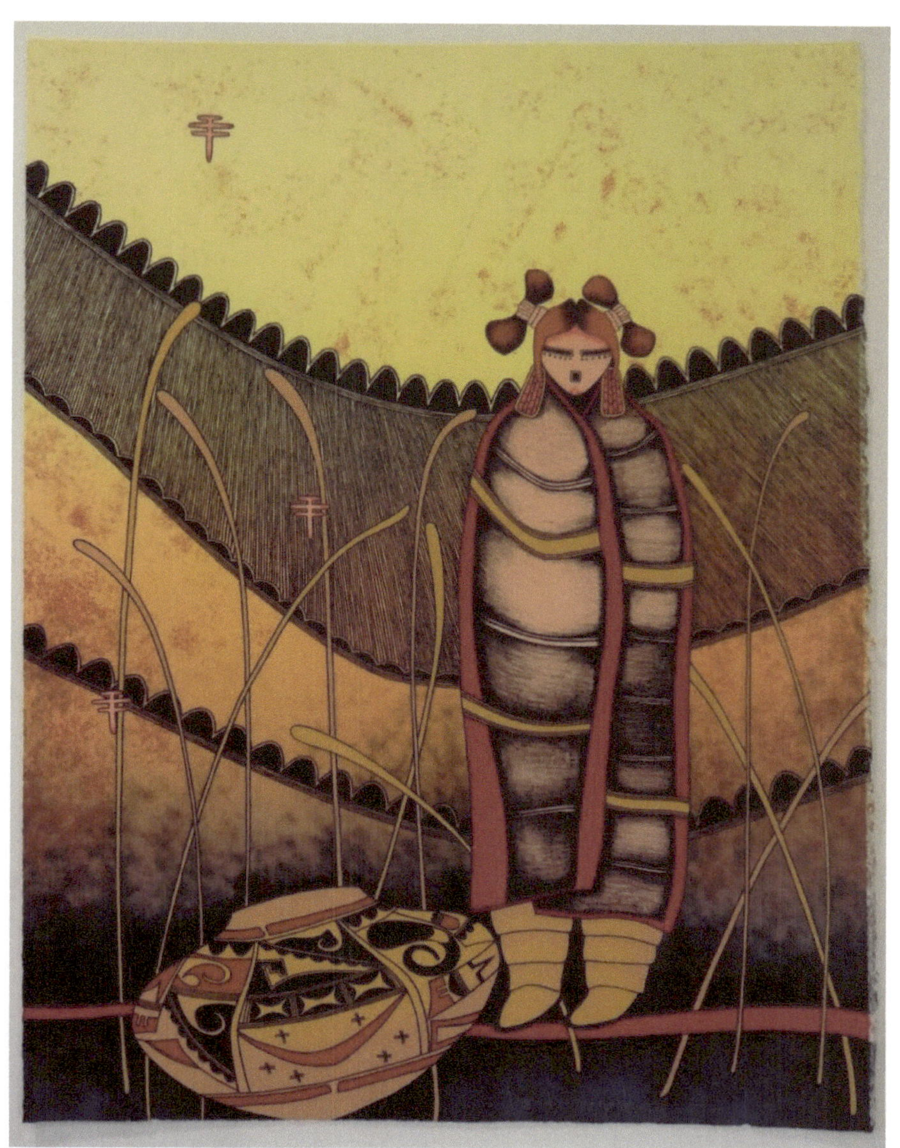

DR 575 - Sunset Song   1985
24" by 18"

Winter Song

Winter Song focuses on the colors of winter. The undulating bands across the background seem to reflect the deepening cold. It is a time of preparation for the seeds and life giving waters which emerge again as the warmth returns.

In this paintings a lovely Hopi potter sings over a Hopi seed jar. She is wrapped in a simple manta and wears traditional white doe-skin moccasins and beautiful earrings. The polychrome seed jar is decorated with typical Sikyatki-revived designs.

The colors of the background are symbolic of the title of the painting. The soft blue to blue-black reflect the emerging cold winter weather. There is a single dragonfly in the upper left corner- a promise of spring. David's water clan affiliation is reflected in the undulating lines in the background, as do the black lines symbolic of rainwater.

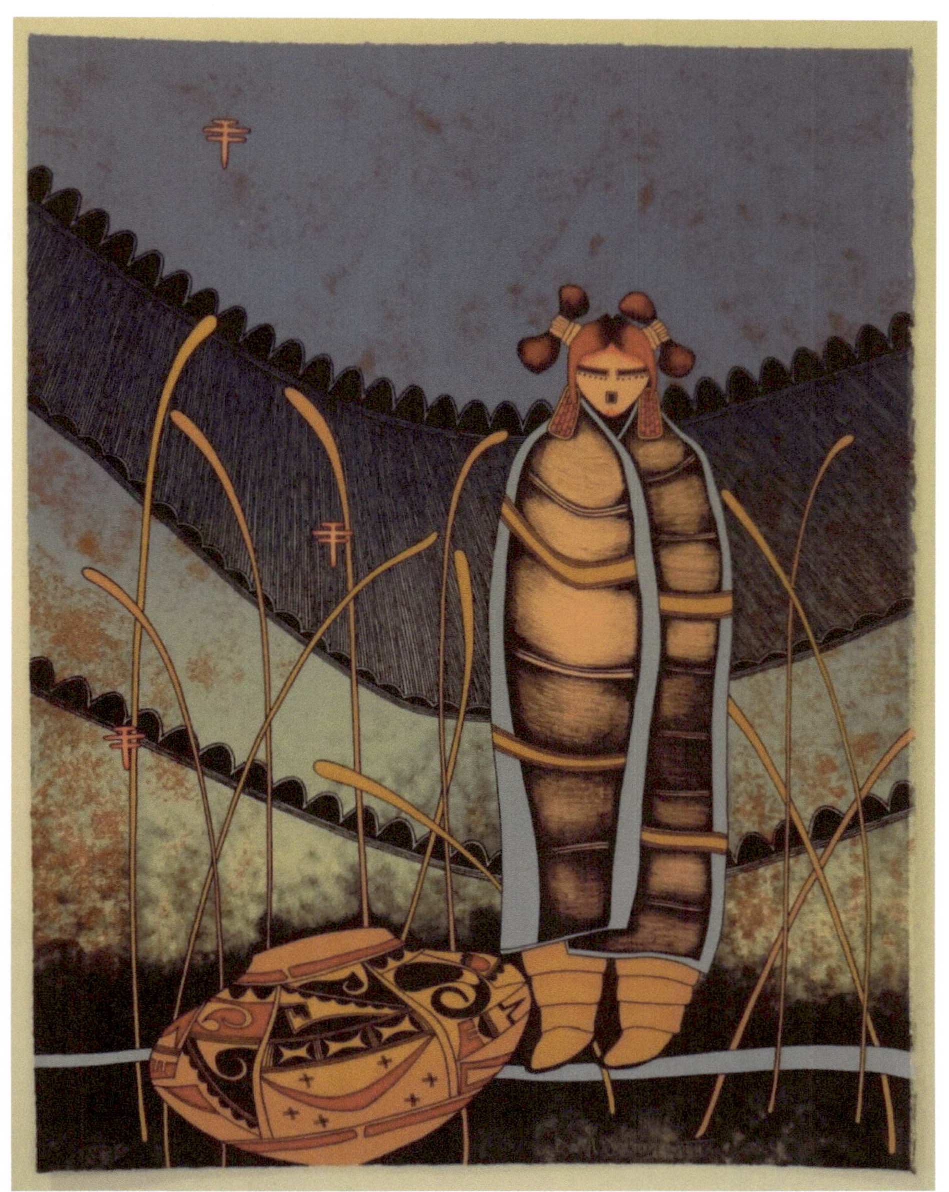

DR 574 - Winter Song   1985
24" by 18"

Turtle Walk

This tranquil image shows a pair of turtles slowly walking through blades of green grass as a beautiful Hopi Sun image looks down on them. The background colors of blue and green are typical of David's Hopi Water Clan.

This original painting is amazingly detailed and very precise with images that flow to the edge of the handmade deckled paper. This painting floats on top of a background mat, so that the entire paper is visible.

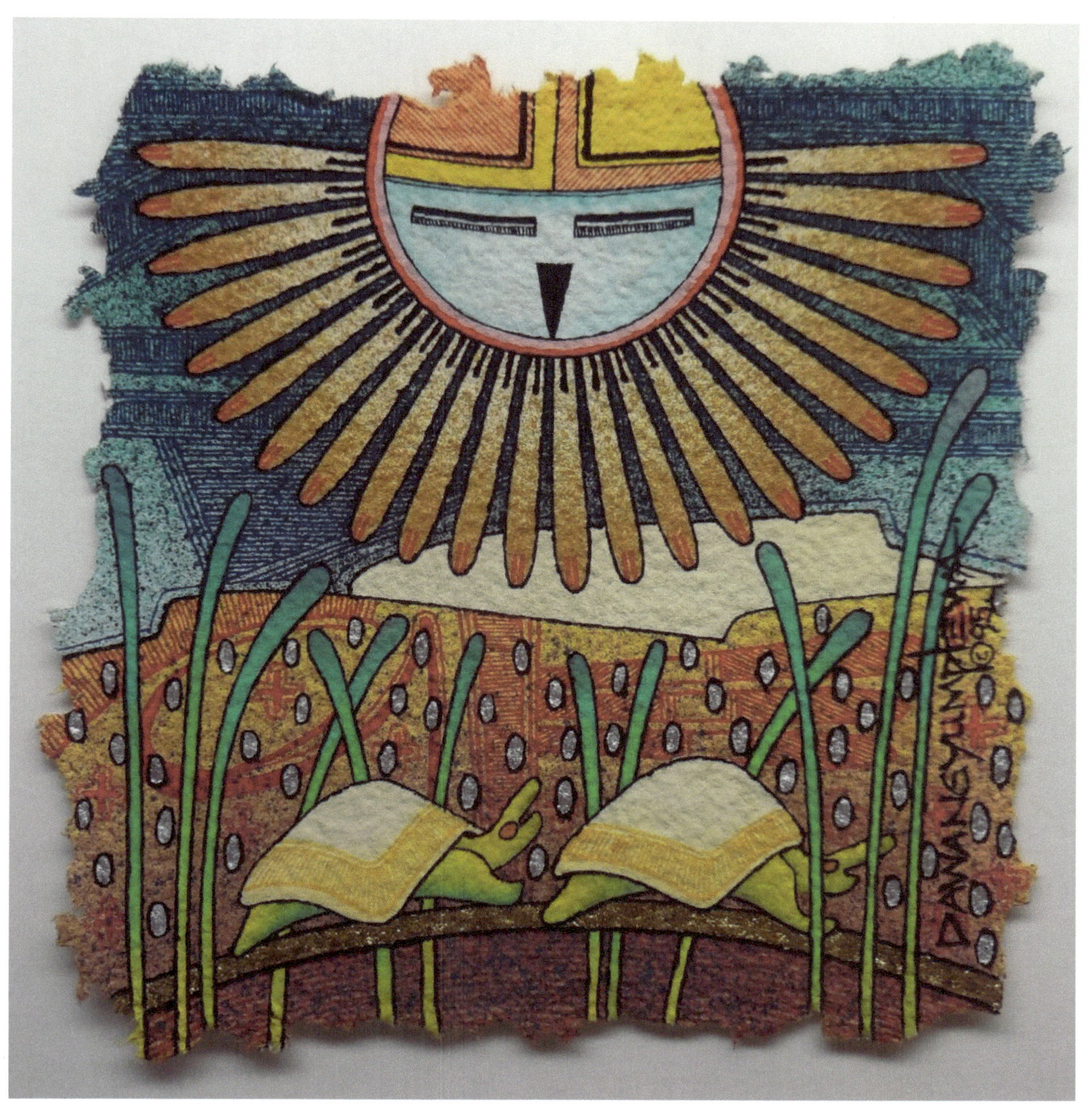

DR 565 - Turtle Walk   1995
                                               6" by 6"

Underwater People

In the Underwater People the contrasting colors and earthen tones depict elements of the earth, the water and the sky. The figures seem to be guarding and protecting the vessels at the bottom and the interspersed crosses, both of which represent life forms. For the Hopi, water brings life and sustenance – whether it is in the form of rain for crops or in the form of aquatic life for food.

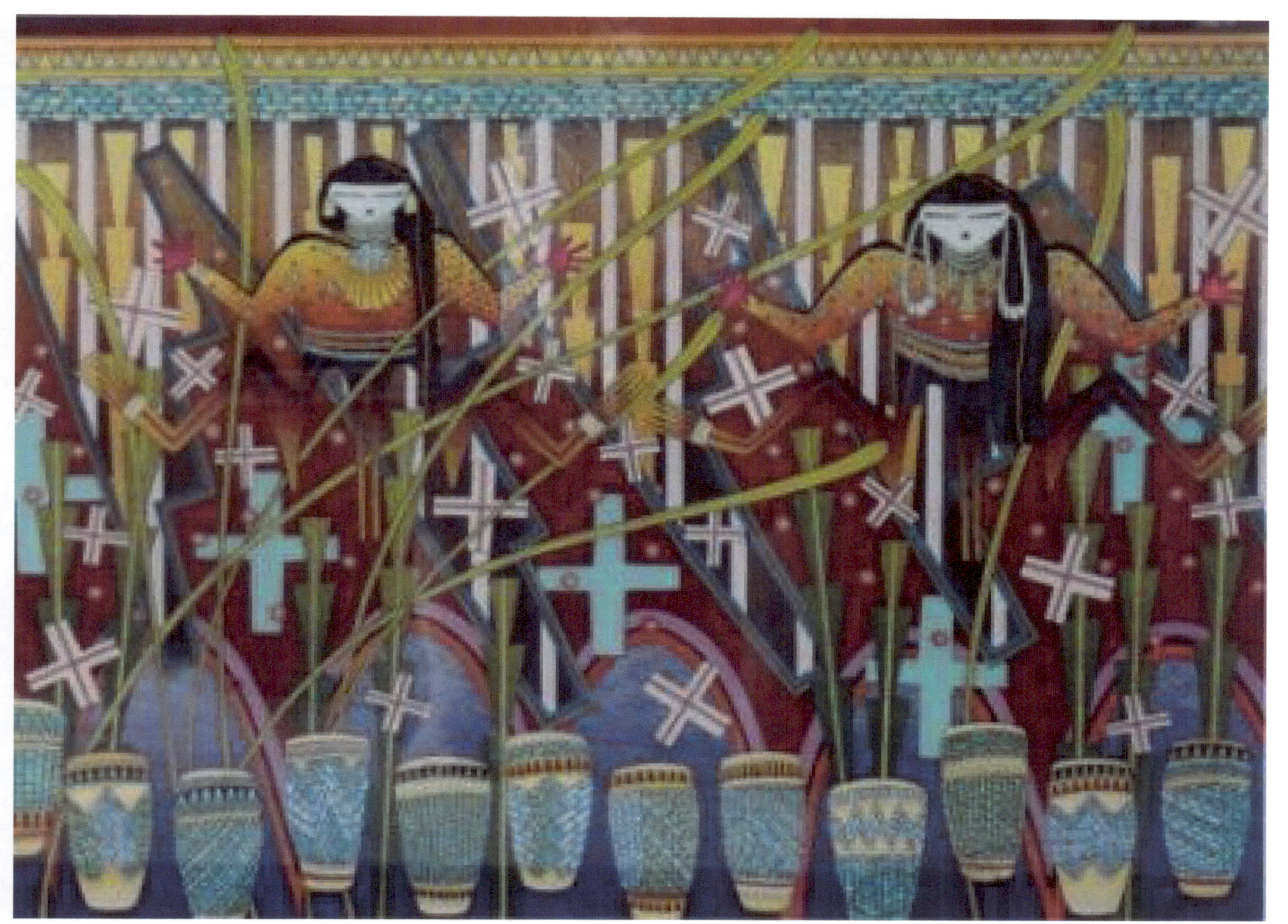

DR 585 - Underwater People   1993
34" x 27 ½" double matted and framed

Sikyatki Girl

"This is an imaginary environment of the village of Sitkyatki on the Hopi Mesas. A water maiden from this village of the yellow house stands among the stylized corn stalks, reeds and the moths in the air.

All of the design elements are symbolic of Water clan imagery. The star crosses and the terraced cloud designs give the boundaries of the above ground blue water drops and the below ground red water droplets.

This long abandoned Hopi village of Sikyatki was the center of the golden age of the pottery that is well known today among collectors of Hopi Pottery." David Dawangyumptewa

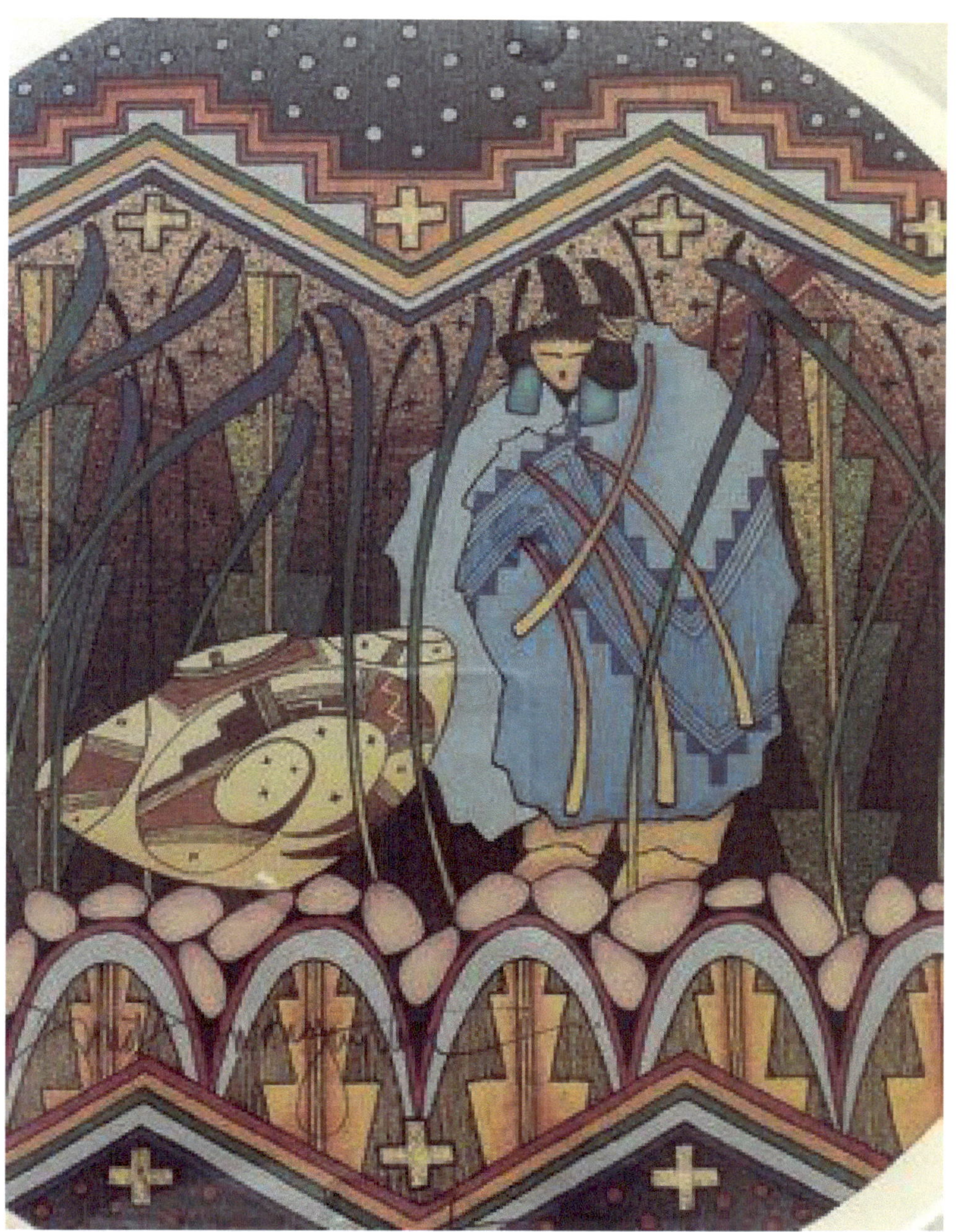

DR 588 Sikyatki Girl   Late 1980s
15" by 15" framed

Singing Potter

This incredible painting was done with gouache paints and 24K gold leaf on handmade deckled edge paper.

The image is of a Hopi potter singing over a Hopi seed jar. She is beautifully dressed in a colorful blanket, traditional white doe-skin moccasins and a pair of large green turquoise earrings.

The polychrome seed jar is decorated with typical Sikyatki-revived designs. David's paintings involve Hopi symbolism, for David is of the Water clan, and jewel like colors. The painting itself is floating on a background mat so that the entire paper is visible and not covered with mat board.

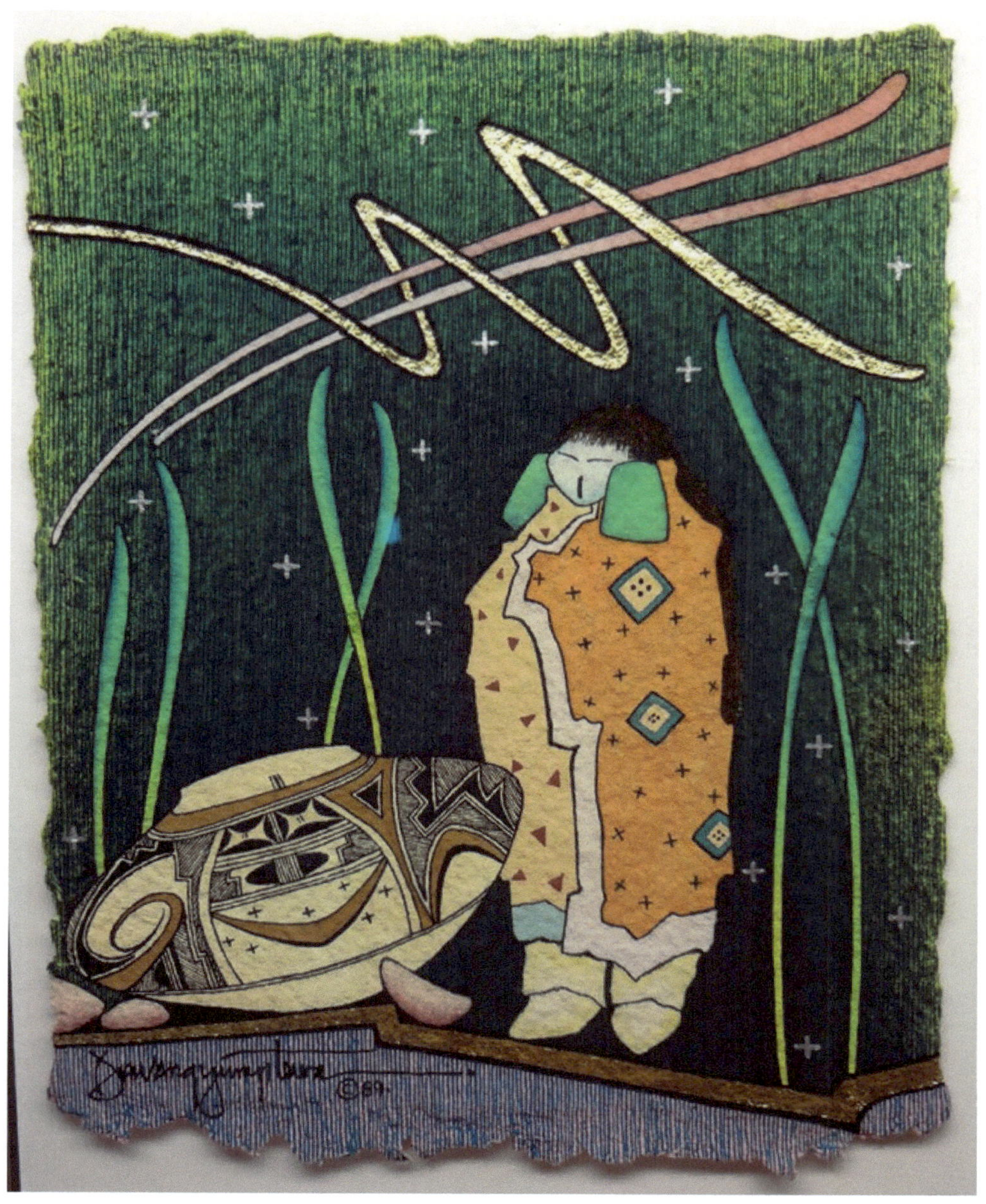

DR 566 - Singing Potter   1989
8 ¾" by 7"

Water Prayers

In this exquisite painting, a Hopi maiden stands by the turtle and frogs, representative of life-giving water. Her mouth is open, indicative of a song or a prayer for the precious liquid.

Two Hopi ollas, used to gather and store water, are in the foreground of the picture. The zig-zag line of silver was hand painted by the artist, and runs through the river as the rain pours down in the back.

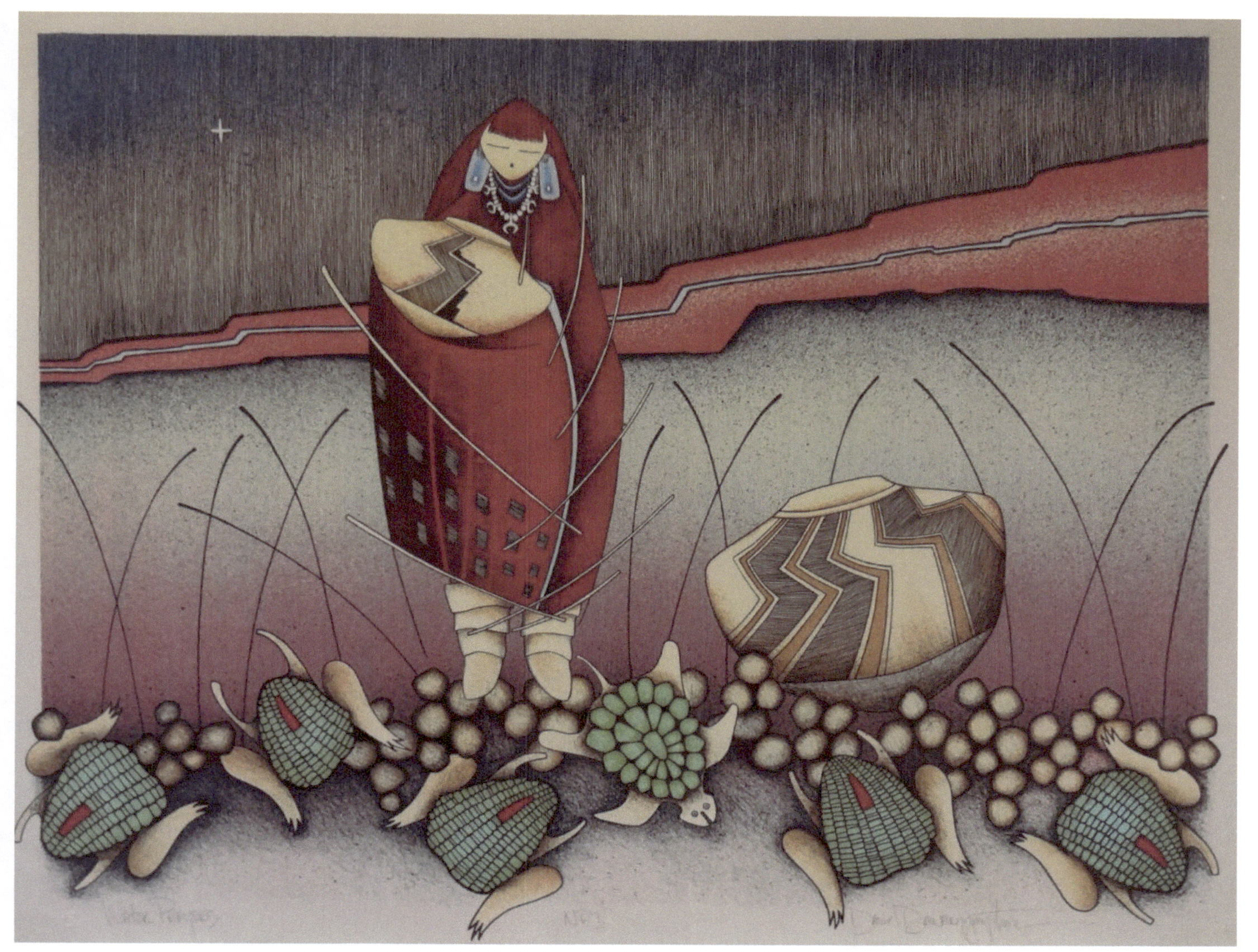

DR 572 - Water Prayers   1986
22 ½" by 28"

Medicine Bundle

For Native Americans, a medicine bundle is private and contains things representative of the most precious of items. It represents a person's spiritual life and may contain powers for protection, healing, good hunting, and even good luck. A medicine bundle may even be passed down through generations as an inheritance.

This incredible painting is very minutely detailed with very fine lines depicting the feathers, background lines and with pieces of turquoise and coral. The striking green circle in the center suggests a new beginning or continued growth- the circle of all life.

Often turquoise is thought of as a healing stone. The feathers seem to indicate the bundle itself, wrapped securely and safely. There are so many layers of meaning represented in the wonderful painting.

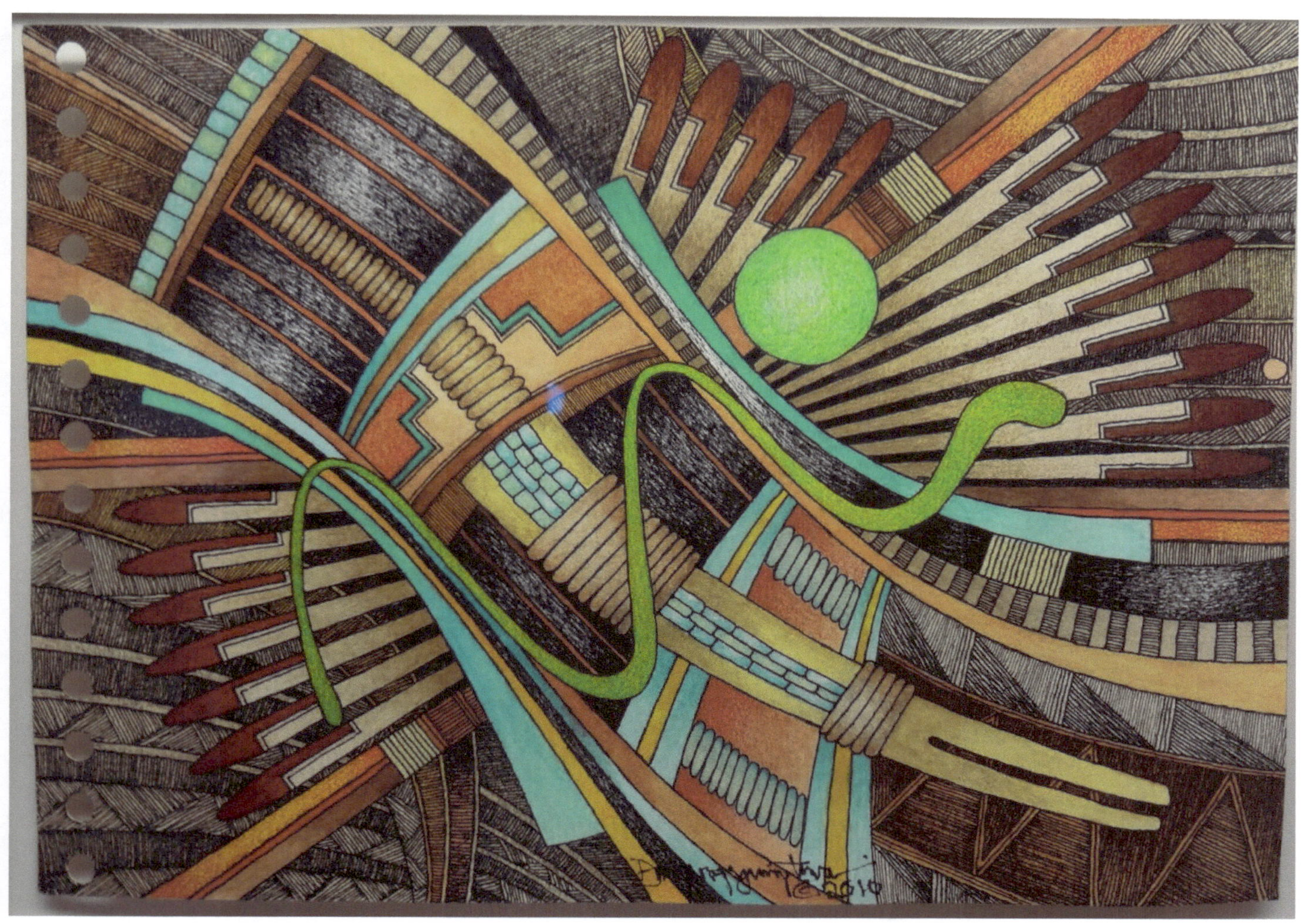

DR 564 - Medicine Bundle   2010
17 ½" by 14 ¾"

Gouache, Pen and Ink

David Dawangyumptewa's colorful mixed media work is simultaneously grounded in tradition and achieves expressive contemporary abstraction.

The style and content of David's work are reflective of his Hopi Background and Water Clan affiliation. His works are abstracted variations of traditional water symbols, frogs, dragonflies and turtles.

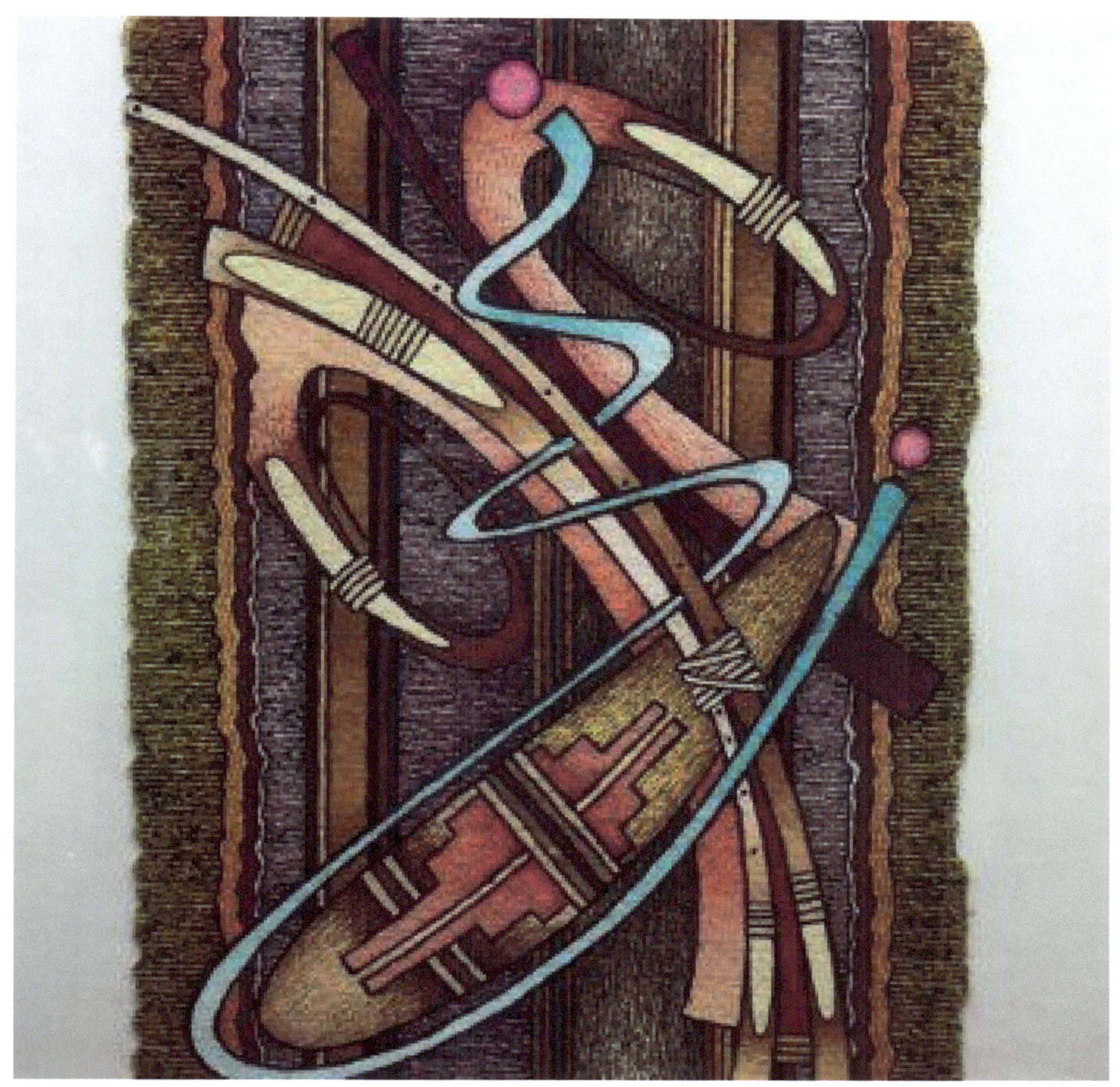

DR 577 - Gouache, Pen and Ink

Circa 2011
7" by 5"

White Buffalo

In many Native American cultures, the White Buffalo is seen as a spiritual message from the Creator for peace, harmony, and a balance among all living things on Mother Earth.

Highly revered, the White Buffalo is very rare, with only one out of approximately 10 million buffalo born with this coloration.

This last piece, *White Buffalo*, was gifted to us by David, and is a very treasured piece of art.

But more than that, we feel that David symbolizes the best elements of the White Buffalo. He is one of the most gentle and caring individuals we have ever met, and those who know him are forever blessed.

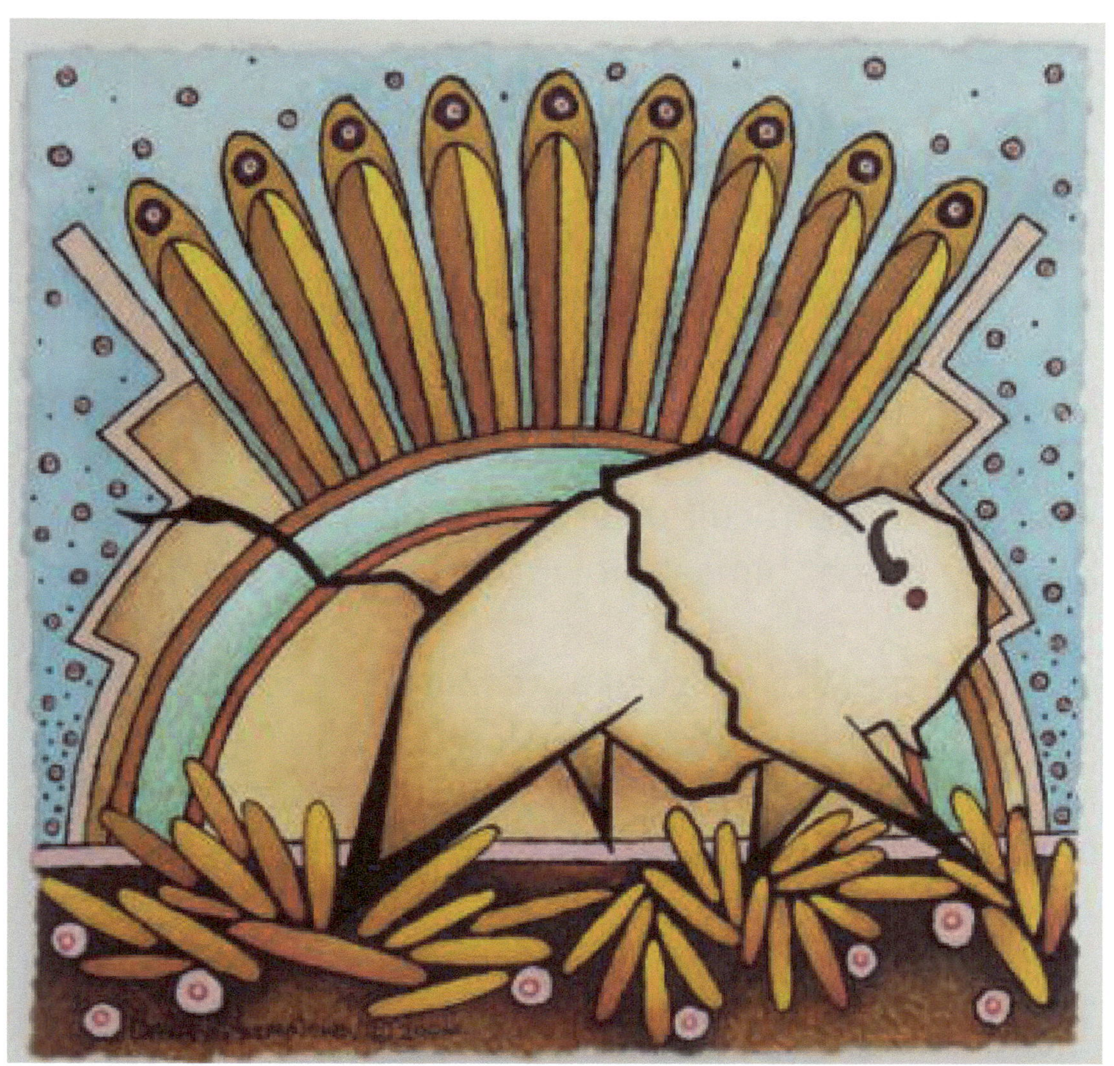

White Buffalo   Circa 2015
                                   6" by 6"

Courage and Perseverance

A little over a decade ago, David suffered a major stroke that cost him the use of the right side of his body.

As a right-handed painter, he could have abandoned his craft and continued through life. But David made the conscious and difficult decision to continue to paint. To do so, he taught himself how to paint with his left hand.

Another aspect of his stroke was his selection of subject matter. His initial works were all people and animal oriented, but after his stroke, his subject matter became more abstract and geometric representations of the Hopi culture.

The stroke took the use of part of his body from him, but David's eye for composition and color remained intact.

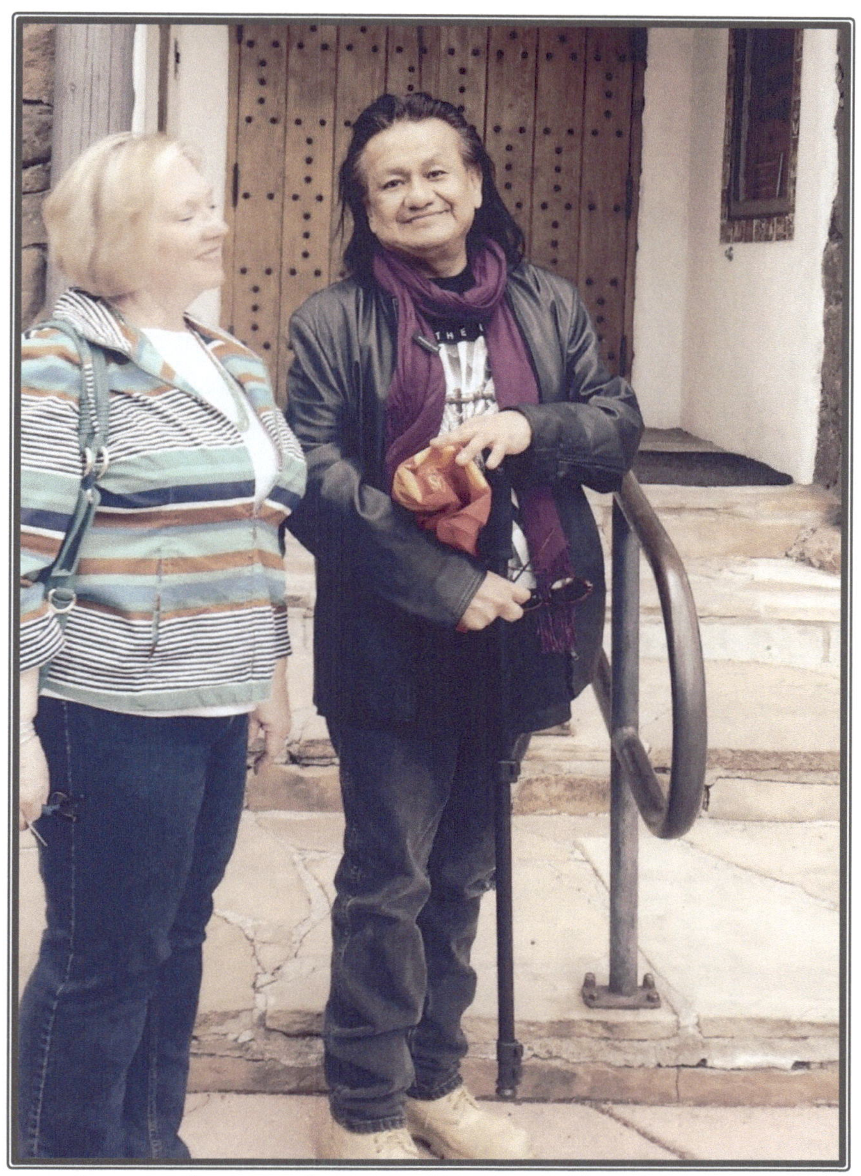

Katie and David
Museum of Northern Arizona
Circa 2016

The Dancing Rabbit Gallery

We certainly hope you enjoyed reading about David Dawangyumptewa and seeing some of his remarkable artwork.

If you wish to acquire any of the pieces featured here, please contact us at:
katie@thedancingrabbitgallery.com

All of the images are copyrighted by the owners of The Dancing Rabbit Gallery unless otherwise attributed.

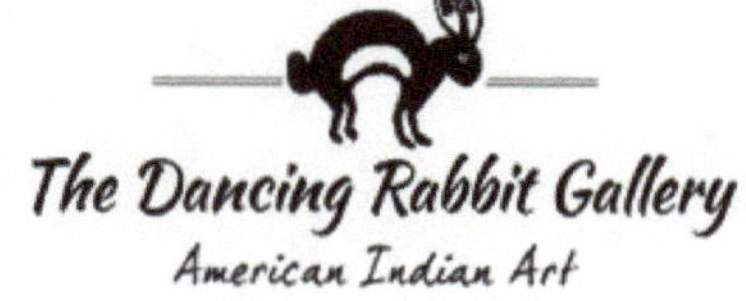

The Dancing Rabbit Gallery
American Indian Art

Founded in 1980 Online since 2012